BIG RIGS ILLUSTRATED

AN AMERICAN LIFESTYLE COLORING BOOK

TEACH

authorHOUSE®

AuthorHouse™
1663 Liberty Drive
Bloomington, IN 47403
www.authorhouse.com
Phone: 1 (800) 839-8640

Published by AuthorHouse 12/14/2018

ISBN: 978-1-5462-7261-8 (sc)
ISBN: 978-1-5462-7260-1 (e)

Library of Congress Control Number: 2018914825

Print information available on the last page.

Any people depicted in stock imagery provided by Getty Images are models,
and such images are being used for illustrative purposes only.
Certain stock imagery © Getty Images.

This book is printed on acid-free paper.

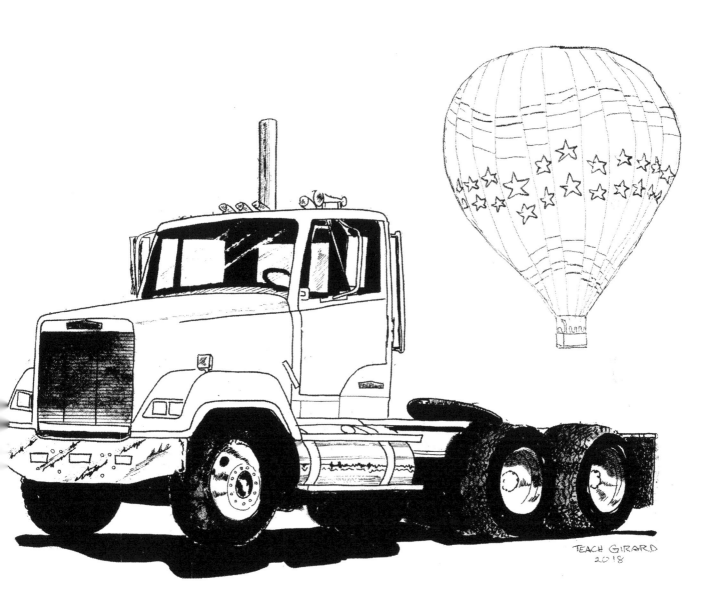

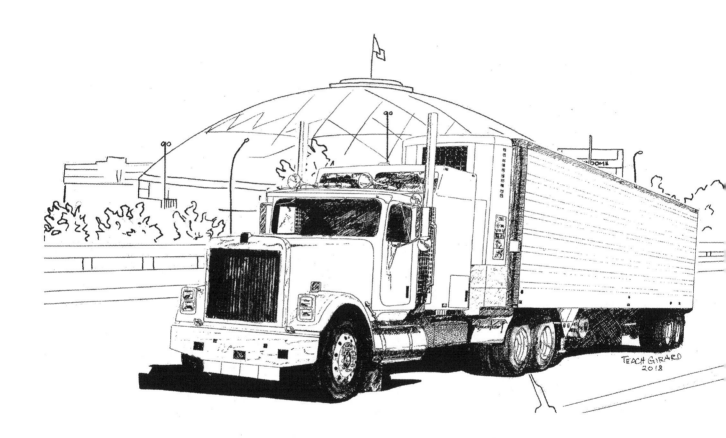

TEACH GIRARD
2018.

TEACH GIRARD
2018

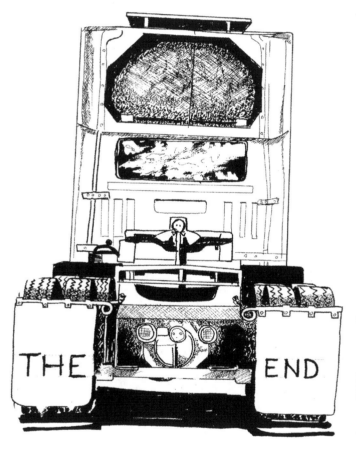

ABOUT THE AUTHOR

John "Teach" Girard

Born and raised in a small town in California. After High School, John joined the United States Air Force in 1964. While serving in the USAF, John acquired a blood clotting disease called thrombophlebitis where the blood was clotting and the veins in his ankles were collapsing resulting in no circulation to the feet.

In 1976 both feet were amputated below his knees. After a medical retirement from the USAF, he went on to college at California State University and University of Oregon to complete his teaching certificate. With the help of his friends he created unique knee controls on his Harley Davidson with a sidecar so he could continue his love for motorcycle riding.

Teach taught arts and crafts in several school districts in Oregon. Now he is living in the Eugene Oregon area with his family where he continues to illustrate transportation-related subjects, such as hot rods, trucks, and motorcycles. His motto defeated but never defeated is tattooed on his arm. He continues to walk on his knees with the help of prosthetic knee pads and a smile and a handshake for folks to see him and thank him for his military service.

Printed in the United States
By Bookmasters